Ladies Wait for God's Chosen Mate

Ms. Brenda Hunter

Publisher: Kingdom News Publication Services, LLC.

DISCLAIMER

All the material contained in this book is provided for educational and informational purposes only. No responsibility can be taken for any results or outcomes resulting from the use of this material.

While every attempt has been made to provide information that is both accurate and effective, the author does not assume any responsibility for the accuracy or use/misuse of this information.

Printed in the United States of America.
ISBN 978-1-955127-28-8

KINGDOM NEWS TODAY
Publication Services, LLC

This is a Christian faith-based book to uplift and encourage single Christian ladies as they are waiting on God and in God to be connected in the marriage of a Holy Matrimony.

2 Corinthians 5:7
"For we walk by faith, not by sight."

PREFACE

Dating Vs Relationship

Before we begin, I want to distinguish the difference between dating and being in a relationship. Often these two terms are used synonymous; however, they are not. Dating is the process of meeting people, collecting data about and getting to know them, but it may not always lead to a relationship. However, when you're in a relationship, a commitment has been made and now you're working towards building a life that includes the two of you moving forward in life.

Once you're in a committed relationship, you begin to discover your partner's imperfections as well as areas where you too need to have developed to be a better mate. Relationships are challenging, but each relationship is different. Just know that difficult times may come at any point within the relationship, but these difficult times can be resolved if the Lord is included as the head of the relationship as well as open communication is being utilized.

As we continue in this little booklet of valuable nuggets to help you prepare to move from being single into a God-focused relationship, the author will share from her heart and personal experiences to help you on your journey.

DEDICATION

I want to dedicate this book to all the single ladies in waiting, every girl, young lady, and woman of all backgrounds and walks of life.

I do have to say that this book was inspired by the trials and errors of my personal life.

My prayer is that the Holy Spirit fills your heart with encouragement, comfort, and peace and that something you read resonates with your willingness to wait in God and on God as He is preparing you to learn to be His only (first) special Lady. To have, to hold, to cherish, to love for life this affair with your First Love (Jesus); He wants to teach us and reach us.

At every waking moment of our lives so we can know Him and the assignments He has created us to fulfill here on earth for Him, His desire is for us to love Him, ourselves and others.

"Therefore, there is now no condemnation for those who are in Christ Jesus." (Romans 8:1 NIV)

So, my dear sister, if you find yourself in a place where you have fallen short as we all do or have done, ask our great Heavenly Father for forgiveness, repent and forgive yourself. Start fresh living your best life in Jesus Name. We must learn from our mistakes and not live in them! AMEN! *"For I know the plans I have for you,"* declares the LORD, *"plans to prosper you and not to harm you, plans to give you hope and a future."* (Jeremiah 29:11 NIV)

Here is a little something to pause, ponder, and pray about:

Dear God, will you give me clarity of your will for my life; am I to be a wife or a satisfied single lady? In Jesus name, I ask. Thank you, God, for your answer. And His answer may be *Yes, No or Wait.*

TABLE OF
CONTENTS

FINDING SELF, SEARCHING WITHIN

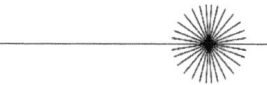

Prayer

Dear God,

My prayer is that the Holy Spirit come and breathe on the pages of this book as the individual reads. I pray you fill them with your loving Spirit and that they feel your arms wrapped around them as in a warm and cozy blanket on a cold winter night or as a breeze refreshing them on a hot summer day. I ask you to lead and guide them to the one you have chosen for them in Jesus' name. Lord, I ask that you give them the wisdom to know if he is real or counterfeit. As a friendship and relationship develops, call them to include you and don't allow any distraction to come, in Jesus' name. Amen!

1

Guard Your Heart

You are a precious jewel, a great valuable prize awaiting to be opened to your set man, The partner God has handpicked just for you to step in the dance with you and your First Love, Jesus Christ.

God will extend your hand to the right man. What is a soulmate? A soulmate is a God-ordained pick for your life that is suitable for your soul and necessary for your assignment.

I encourage you as a single lady to keep a gate around your heart (Proverbs 4:23) and to keep your heart with all diligence, for out of it springs the issues of life.

Remember to date from your mind, not your heart. The heart and mind are connected, and each have their own distinct purposes. The heart and mind are mentioned several times in the Bible. When speaking of the heart, it often refers to how we control our desires, emotions, hopes, dreams, and other intangible areas of our inner man, whereas the mind refers to intellect, reasoning, and thoughts.

The heart and mind are needed to walk by faith because the Bible instructs us to trust and believe. To believe, we must engage our minds while to trust we must depend on our heart.

Therefore, guard your heart with your life. Do not stir up nor awaken love until it pleases (Song of Solomon 8:4). In other words, until the set time ordained by God. He will direct your path.

When you lose your valuable time, you can't get it back. You may want some company, but God wants you to have some help.

He who finds a wife (Proverbs 18:22)—ladies, it's not your job to find, but to be found. Don't let circumstances of loneliness distract you and push you out of the role God has established. When Boaz found Ruth, she was working and minding her business and taking care of her family, so remember you don't have to run after a man whether rich or poor (Ruth 3:10).

If you are following God's directions, He will put you where you need to be, to be found. You won't be found if you are hanging out at home, so go out and enjoy life, and as you're enjoying life, you just may be found.

When two souls connect, blessings flow not only for the people in the relationship, but those connected to them. It's important to build a relationship with someone suitable for your soul and necessary for your assignment.

If you and your mate are not compatible or spiritually yoked, building a life pleasing to God will be difficult. Allow God to lead you on your journey; don't pick for yourself. Fast, pray and seek God.

Once someone enters your life, take your time, and don't rush. Observe their values and behaviors because the one who is right for you should have values that align with your needs, and they should complement you. This individual should push you closer to God and not distract you or discourage you from the things of God. They should not interfere with your assignment; they should support it and help to advance it. Their values should meet your needs.

It seems that most people don't know what they need until they are in a relationship and not getting desired results. We don't always know ourselves and then we want someone to see us as whole. How do we expect others to see us as something specific when we don't even know ourselves or even what it is we need or desire? In your singleness, learn who you are and what makes you your best person, so that you are able to communicate effectively with your mate.

DO YOU TRUST GOD ENOUGH TO BE LONELY FOR A SEASON?

We should trust God with our happiness. Don't just settle for happiness when you can experience joy—unexplainable and peaceable joy. Know that God is our source, and He knows everything about us and everything that will fulfill our life's purpose, so learn to depend on Him and not what you feel you need. Remember, the devil will work with all his might to deceive you, so if you connect with someone, you must seek the Lord to ensure that the man is sent by God and not from a place of evil because if he's not from God, it could bring turmoil.

Think of yourself and value the woman that you are. You are a woman of worth, and it is very important that you wait on God. Waiting on God and in God for a mate that's right for you will bring a man who adds to your life and does not take away or hinder what you already have established. You don't want just anyone, nor somebody who's playing games; you want someone who's mature, a man after God's heart and seeking His guidance. You want a relationship that is Christ-centered, so if you're waiting and your mate is seeking, God will point you to one another. Your foundation in Christ that each of you possess is like what the Bible speaks of when it refers to *iron sharpens iron*.

In order to not be unequally yoked, it is best to be in a relationship with someone spiritually enlightened and down-to-earth. You may have some fear of being hurt, but I encourage you to wait for the one God has for you. God's chosen for you will be one that respects you and will be in touch with your emotions.

As mentioned earlier, the devil will try to counterfeit and send someone your way who looks good and sounds good but ends up not being the right one. Be careful and don't waste your time with someone who will take advantage of you. A healthy relationship will be a balanced relationship. People value the things they work for. The one coming is willing to wait with you, and for you; your outcome will come from you guarding your heart.

For a good strong foundation, you have to build upon your relationship in the proper order. So many times, in relationships that aren't established where God is not a factor, lines get crossed and things progress in an order that is not ordained by God. Intimacy cannot be a foundation for your relationship. A physical relationship introduces strongholds and soul ties that can stay with you for many years beyond a failed relationship. The best foundation to establish a relationship is a spiritual one. Learn if your potential mate has a relationship with God and their views and commitment to following Christ. Once this is established, then learn more about what makes them who they are, their experiences with family, childhood experiences, etc. Then there must be a commitment stage where a decision is made that this person is your person and you continue to build. You want to identify this person's personality, likes, dislikes, triggers, etc. It is during this time of discovery that you begin to learn their love languages and the things they need to feel and receive the love you are offering.

Instead of being the first stage in a relationship, physical intimacy is the final stage to build on. This is an area where the enemy will tease you and tempt you; please don't fall into his web and trap. You are not a car; you don't have to go on a test ride, if you know what I'm talking about. Don't make it easy for him because eventually, he will realize you are more than your beauty, and your booty. He will find out from the Holy Spirit that you are the whole package made just for him.

God is a master mechanic and is flawless in His work, but the enemy will have you thinking you need to submit to being taken for a test ride just to see if you are sexually compatible. You don't want to play; you want the one who wants to wait to open the prize, the one who sees you as a precious jewel and works for the reward. PRAISE THE LORD!

Sometimes we should let go of what we want for what we need. God loves you, and He loves the concept of waiting for Him and on Him. Protect your heart, and don't let anyone play with it.

BE A NON-COMPROMISING WOMAN OF GOD

I know some of you reading this now are saying, "Man, Ms. Brenda, you keep on talking about guarding your heart." I am stressing this because, for some of us, it takes a lifetime to heal. In the natural, the heart is a vital organ for which life flows, and the same is in the spiritual. It is to be guarded for your wellbeing.

There may be times in life when God will remove someone or something from your life. When God does this—and it could be because it was never ordained by Him or this person or thing was out of order for your life—you must understand who you are and whose you are. If you are a child of God; He will watch out for you and protect you. Listen for His voice and allow Him to have dominion over your thoughts.

You just can't date or hook up with anybody. Be submitted to God's authority, and He will multiply your life. Sometimes you must close doors to have new doors opened.

Wait on the Lord, be of good courage, and He shall strengthen your heart (Psalm 27:14). This true love who awaits you is the beginning of great success. Your set man is coming in divine timing. Patience, the ability of waiting for something (or in this case, someone) without getting angry or upset is a virtue. Submitting to God's way of doing things is vital.

At times, you may feel lonely and may want to get upset because you don't have someone, but don't let your guard down and don't take steps backward from what you know God desires of you.

FORGIVENESS

Before the time comes, if there be any unforgiveness within your heart, repent and forgive others and yourself. Unforgiveness will cause many hindrances. Forgiving others in past relationships is important because without forgiveness you may be on guard for new relationships which may become a hindrance. Also, forgiving yourself is most important because you are the person, you're with 100% of the time. There is no such thing as taking a break from yourself. You can take a break from a significant other, your kids, etc., but never yourself. So, since you're always with you, you must learn to always forgive yourself. Use your mistakes as a way of learning and moving forward. Our mistakes are to be learned from, not lived in.

In a relationship where true love has developed and marriage is possible, see it as a fresh start in your life. Keep moving forward, and don't hold yourself back with negative things or unforgiveness; stay positive and strong for your soulmate connection. Leave behind people who didn't deserve you. *"Brethren (Sisters), I do not count myself to have apprehended; but one thing I do, forgetting those things which are behind and reaching forward to those things which are ahead."* (Philippians 3:13) You can't win a race looking back; unforgiveness is like always looking backwards while trying to progress forward. Continuing to look back will make you miss what's ahead for you.

Always recognize your powers and strengths. There's a beautiful new beginning you need for this new balance to continue forward. Healing from the past must take place, and we must cut toxicity from our lives. Sometimes, that means to cut people.

Allow God to guide you, and don't be afraid to shine. Allow yourself to connect with your soulmate. You will make solid decisions if you have clarity; so, when you feel that you are struggling with something, go to

God in prayer and ask for understanding, wisdom, and clarity in this situation.

What the enemy meant for harm, God will use for your advantage and the good (Genesis 50:20). While in the midst of a situation, you may not feel good will ever come, but God is able to turn the worst of things around for the good. Know that various things have already happened, so stand strong in your decision and believe that your soulmate may just be delayed. Remember, God must clear a path so things can be put in order before you both come together. Strength comes by being patient and waiting on the Lord, so don't get weary in your waiting. You are doing well!

Just as you may be going through a process of healing, he too may be experiencing similar things. Each of you may need to go through a purging process to be released before you can come together. Don't be fearful of change; be fully open to receiving your good gift.

Take it slow; you can have an abundant life on your journey and enjoy each other's company.

As you are the lady waiting, rediscover who you are. Know the temperature of your heart, believe that you are a great treasure, know your power and ask God to show you the heart of the man in your preparation season as you await your sent man. Keep the faith that your soulmate is coming at the set time. You will know him when you see him.

FROM THE AUTHOR'S HEART

Beloved, my prayer to you all is that God gives you the desires of your heart.

WHEN THINGS DON'T LOOK RIGHT, GOD HAS A PLAN

Prayer

Dear God,

Lord, help me to separate myself from anything that is not holy. I don't want to waste my life on things that have no value. Give me discernment to recognize that which is worthless and remove myself from it. Help me not to give myself to impure things, but rather to those things that fulfill Your plans for my life. In Jesus' name, Amen!

Ladies, choose holiness over happiness. God gives us a blueprint to be followed by following the red lettering of His Word. When Jesus speaks in parables, He is giving us instruction and guidance on how to handle life's challenges. If we learn to reflect on the words of Jesus, we will be able to identify people and things that are good for us as well as people and things that are not good for us. The red letters within the scriptures will help us identify the red flags in our lives. It will help us to see if that man who is trying to entertain our time is sent by God to find you or a distraction to keep you from obtaining the one God has prepared for you.

We cannot serve two masters. If God is truly our Lord and Master, we will desire to please Him above all others. If pleasing people is your goal, you will be enslaved to them. People can be harsh taskmasters, so be careful not to give them power over you.

INTIMACY WITH THE LORD

If I am the master of your life, says the Lord, I will also be your First Love. Serving the Lord is rooted and grounded in His vast unconditional love for you.

Know that the lower you bow down before Him, the higher your intimate relationship with Him develops. The joy of living in His presence outshines all other pleasures. Take time to reflect on His joyous light by living in increased intimacy with the Father (Matthew 6:24, Revelations 2:4, Ephesians 3:16-17 and Psalm 16:11).

WHEN YOU FALL INTO TEMPTATION

The devil is always trying to challenge your good intentions and make you fall. If he can make you turn from your declared devotion to the Lord, he is happy. It is a way of him being able to mock God. Remember the story of Job: the devil was trying to bring all these challenges against Job so that he would mock God, but Job was upright and steadfast in his trust in God. We must have the same tenacity when it comes to the things of God in our own lives.

At this time, I desire to share a transparent moment of my life with you to better help you. My desire is to be pleasing to the Father at all times, but there was a time several years ago that I was not as strong in my waiting. I fell for Satan's tricks, and I opened the door to the spirit of lust. I let my guard down and entered an intimate relationship with a man, knowing deep inside that he was not the one God sent for me. Those few moments of pleasure may have felt good at the moment, but it cost me much more. I was consumed with guilt and shame and had so many internal feelings that I had to deal with.

When I was in this storm, I did not see that I was blind-sided by the deceiver. That's why it's so important for us to watch as well as pray and set good godly standards.

The healing process was very difficult, but glory be to God, He never left me. The awesome thing about our God who loves us unconditionally is that even though we may disappoint Him and stray from Him, He never leaves us. Now that I'm on the other side and healed, God has made me stronger. I am forever grateful for His grace and His mercy.

Your personal and intimate relationship with the Lord will help you to be non-compromising in your actions. Be determined to be a non-compromising woman of God.

In my quest to please the Lord, I have not yet met that special someone who's willing to date me long enough to respect the Christ in me and abstain from acts that are not pleasing to the Lord. I am determined to wait in God and on God and to receive the blessings He has in store for me because of my wait.

I trust the Lord and believe that He keeps His promises. I believe He will Give us the desire of our hearts in his timing.

FEELINGS OF REJECTION

I believe the happiest people in the world are those who hang on to what God says and follows His word. Don't hold on to somebody who doesn't see your value or your worth. Your value is not to be shared with everyone, just that one special somebody that God is preparing just for you. Man's rejection is God's direction and His great protection.

Dr. N. Cindy Trimm says, "Rejection is a divine announcement that those persons can no longer prosper you and that it's time to move on and that you didn't move on quick enough, so the rejection happened. It's also a sign that that person no longer has the capacity to support your purpose and your destiny." She goes on to admonish people to not cry because of the rejection, but to throw yourself a going away party" (*Cindy Trimm Ministries*).

COMPATIBILITY

To be compatible with someone, both partners learn to understand and accept the other's life philosophies and goals. There comes a time when they genuinely enjoy being around one another, and when the other is not present there is a void, and they begin to miss the other person. Respect becomes important to one another, and a level of protection is established between the two of them.

All relationships are imperfect, and there may be some disagreements from time to time. The fact that you have an argument is not that big of an issue. No two people are going to see eye to eye 100% of the time. However, the main thing to watch for is the behaviors displayed during an argument. If the behaviors move beyond a level of respect and the fighting no longer seems to be fair, then it's time to assess the compatibility or incompatibility of one another in the relationship.

Ladies, remember you are a jewel, but you must operate with a level of respect towards your mate. Mutual compatibility is rare, and if he's willing to let you walk away like he doesn't want you, sometimes it's best to go ahead and walk away instead of fighting for something that is in a continual state of toxicity. Toxic relationships bring added stress in one's life. Again, remember, ladies, man's rejection is God's direction and protection.

Some men want to have the benefits of you without loving you. When a man truly loves you, he will do what he must to make you feel loved by showing you love and doing special things for you. He will look for love inside you and let love surprise you. Just because he is doing all these kind things, now is not the time to let your guard down; continue to pray and seek God's approval for this relationship. God should be in all your business. Can we get an Amen?

As you receive God's approval, now is the time to get busy in doing you as a lady of contentment. As your sent one is making you feel special and expressing to you how he feels about you and you sharing your feelings about him, be honest and build a firm foundation of trust and honesty. Just know that a man who's not willing to commit will make you an option, not a priority.

CONTENTMENT

Ladies, here are some of the things I've learned as I wait on God and in God. I've learned to be content. I've learned to seek God and ask Him, "What is it that I can accomplish today in my waiting? Are my actions in this season pleasing to you, God? God, what can I do for you today as your servant?"

Focusing on serving in His kingdom and serving the Lord daily is what keeps me grounded and rooted in Him. I realized that I need to keep open lines of communication with God to succeed in my waiting season. While single, learn that your relationship with your First Love (Jesus) is priority. Enjoy that intimacy with the Father and relish every moment.

During this time of singleness, seek the Father on ways to incorporate your mate into the equation once he appears. The Lord will begin to groom you to be the mate He desires you to be.

Manifestation

God is faithful, and He will give you the desires of your heart. Know that the longer you wait, the better it gets. It may not seem like it but trust the process. God will put His manifestation in a man of God right before you when it's time.

When it's time for the sent man to pursue you, it's not a problem for God. Put in the work of what you ask for; don't give more of yourself to someone who is not worthy of having you. The sent man will respect your relationship with the Lord. The man God sends will appreciate and celebrate you and Love You Out Loud! He will let everyone know just how much he loves you.

Establish and communicate your priorities and make appropriate time to spend with your companion. There is a time and season for all things, so you don't have to neglect your relationship with the Lord and just focus all your waking hours on your mate.

Before your mate comes, stop focusing on when he will come and what he will look like and what it will be like to be around him. Focus on you and Jesus. Don't allow the fantasies to cloud your vision and take dominion over your relationship with Christ.

THE RIGHT CONNECTION

The Bible shares that we should not be equally yoked with unbelievers (2 Corinthians 6:14). This biblical reference is referring to two oxen joined by a wooden bar to complete work together. If oxen are unequal, they are not equal in strength, with one being weaker. This imbalance will cause difficulties in completing the task before them.

Let's now look at this analogy from a Christian living perspective. If a believer in Christ is yoked to an unbeliever, then the believer will not be able to adequately live out the Christian life God desires them to live. The unbeliever (weaker vessel) is living their life according to the flesh, which may hinder the believer.

Remember, the right man, the one sent from God, will have some things in common with you, and God will be your foundation to getting to know one another. As we walk this faith walk of believing God for our sent mate, we must remember that our faith is not meant to associate with the darkness of this world, which confirms that we cannot be unequally yoked to a non-believer.

NOW OR FOREVER

People come into your life for a reason or a season, so when the next man enters your life, ask God, *Why did he come?* Sometimes God uses people to shake us up to see if your foundation is strong and to teach us and bring us closer to Him. Being grounded and rooted in the things of God will help you live a more fulfilled life.

Just know that God is in your life forever and will never leave you nor forsake you. He desires to be included in every part of our lives, so while you're waiting in God and on God, nurture your relationship with Him. He knows what we need, even before we know what we need. He has promised to provide all that abundantly. We are fearfully and wonderfully made by Him, so allow your sense of security to rest in Him. Humans will disappoint you and let you down, so do not rest on having someone else to make you happy. Rest on the promises of God. Don't lean on your own understanding, but learn to trust in the Lord with all your heart and always acknowledge Him (Proverbs 3:5-6). Allow Him to direct your path. He will direct that sent man on that path to find you. So, ladies, it's time to go out and become "lost" so that you may be "found."

God is training you to depend on Him while you are single. Teaching you to be content in His presence alone with Him. He is teaching us discipline and self-control over our desires and flesh by being under the submission of the Holy Spirit. A strong relationship with Him will stop us from just going out to get into something and end up in a place of temptation. Don't move until you know it's God's direction for your protection.

I'M BEING PREPARED

There's nothing better than God's Timing. Do more praying for your future husband than thinking of him. Love and intimacy are more than sex. Take this time of being single to learn yourself, love yourself, and date yourself. It is so important to know what makes us who we are because when you add another person to the equation, things get more complicated. We need to know how our inner man responds and reacts, and we must learn self-control over our responses.

The person you're waiting on will be your biggest influence and the one you will spend the rest of your life with. In the beginning, all things will be blissful, but what about after the "honeymoon phase" has come to an end? Those things that used to be "cute" can become downright annoying. What are you going to do? How are you going to respond and communicate? In relationships, you need to learn to pick your battles, so is that annoying little trait something to bring up or do you just pray for the strength to see past it? Do you want to be right, or do you want to be in love in your relationship? Love covers a multitude of sin (1 Corinthians 13).

In your waiting, God is preparing. He's not only preparing your mate, but He's preparing you. Because just as you are praying and seeking the Lord to be found by the one, He created for you, your future mate too is praying and seeking the Lord.

So, find your best self because God is working on both of you so you can be ready at the same time in your right mindset, being on one accord and equally yoked.

When the sent one comes, continue to pray. Also, don't take their word, but look at their actions. In time, people's actions will show you who they are. They can tell you anything, but their actions speak much louder than any words. Observe their character. Observe how they treat others. Their fruits and true intentions will be revealed. So don't rush things because if it's meant to be, you have a lifetime to walk this journey.

Remember, you are to be found, and if he wants you, he will pursue you and wait with you. Get to know the man standing up before you know him lying down. Position yourself in the right standings. Don't lie or lay, and don't play—you are of value!

FROM THE AUTHOR'S HEART

Ladies, you are enough; you are complete by yourself. Take each lesson from God to know who He created you to be. You want to be 100% ready at all times just being you and who He created you to be.

FAITH WILL KEEP YOU

Prayer

Dear Father,

I trust you with all the details in this waiting transition season of my life. I trust you at your word. You are taking me from glory to glory. Thank you!

Help me to surrender to your hand and not be tempted to move too swiftly out of the spiritual growing pains. Thank you for your grace that covers me here in the stillness of life. In my waiting season, God, if you want me to be alone, I ask you, Dear God, to take away the loneliness. In Jesus' name, I pray Amen.

Ladies, as we continue our journey of waiting on God and in God, rest in God's purpose and His provision of grace. We declare and decree we are loved today, not despised.

The foundation of our faith is developed in the waiting room of life. It is often done behind the scenes and in the "not quite-yet" season of your life. Don't get discouraged during these times because this is where God is preparing that special person just for you. Your chosen one is getting ready for this wonderful union to take place in God's timing.

It's in a transition time where God is developing your perseverance and purifying your motives. He is transforming the inside for what's about to happen on the outside.

I have learned to know that the devil will strike even harder when he hears you say you're waiting for God. He finds rocks to throw and tries to hide his hands. That's why it's so important for us to watch and pray because the deceiver will speak your love language. He will send a counterfeit, Ismael, to whisper lies into your ear. He wants to bring distraction so he will sound and look like the real thing, but we must always test the spirit and know the fruit of the tree.

Always stay connected with your First Love (Jesus) and do not cheat on your husband, which is God until your earthen-sent man appears. We are assured and know that God is a partner in our labor of waiting for all things will work together and fitting into a plan for good for those who love God and are called according to His design and purpose. (*Ms. Brenda's emphasis added to the above reading from Romans 8:28.*)

"Let's cast all our anxiety on Him because He cares for us," (1 Peter 5:7) *"and be anxious for nothing but in everything by prayer and supplication, with thanksgiving, let your request be made known to God: and the peace of God which surpasses all understanding will guard your hearts and minds through Christ Jesus."* (Philippians 4:6-7). *"For we walk by faith, not by sight."* (2 Corinthians 5:7)

When you live with an open heart, unexpected, joyful things happen. It's tempting in the waiting transition to say there isn't much taking place, but as you know God is working things out behind the scenes for our good. Look for the blessings by reaping the benefit of your waiting transition.

Don't be in desperation; just be real with the Lord about the desires of your heart. Be more present with your family, friends, and loved ones, and be honest with them.

MY GIFT TO YOU

Ladies, I would like to share how Prophetess Tashielia Hunter spoke a word to me about how God is giving me a personal love letter to share with you single ladies. I'm grateful God is speaking clearly to us, and I ask God to search my heart so I can be more watchful over it. As I pray and as the woman of God was prophesying to me, God gave me a new revelation. He began to show me that as I share this message with you, I too must eat at the buffet for myself. He said, "You do it first."

The word that was received told me that I must be a better watchman over the doors of my heart and that I need to ask God to reveal the temperature of my heart in each season. I was instructed to stand guard because the enemy will come to try and steal, kill, and destroy what God is preparing you for.

The Holy Spirit continued to tell me to watch out for all the fiery darts. God is establishing you in the

32

waiting, and the Holy Spirit will allow you to see the wisdom of the mysteries of God as we continue to eat daily at the buffet (The Bible). You will learn how to keep the deceiver out by being in the word daily!

Let the sent man find you in doing God's business and don't open the doors of your heart for a stranger. The Bible tells us, "...Do not stir up or awaken love until it pleases..." (Song of Solomon 8:4). In other words, until God's set timing or until the appropriate time.

Keep your ears tuned to the teaching of the Holy Spirit. Even when the devil is talking, the teacher will give you all the answers, praise be to God. This is an open book test; you can do it because all the answers are already provided for you... HALLELUJAH!

FROM THE AUTHOR'S HEART

Don't give away 30 years for 30 minutes of pleasure. Rest in your salvation, and don't lay it down for one night of pleasure that will cause you a lifetime of pain and a mind stretched by every new experience. Once an area is explored, it can never go back to its old dimensions. Walk in the peace of God, for He will quicken you.

DON'T HIDE
YOUR LIGHT

Prayer

Dear God,

Thank you for opening my eyes to the truth of your grace. Please keep me filled with your Spirit, so that your wisdom may never depart from me. May your truth grow deep roots within my heart, and will you open my eyes and mind to always discerning and watchful for temptations and lies that would try to steal your truth away from me.

Hide your light within me so that I may not sin against you. I ask this in the name of Jesus. Amen!

Best Kept Secret

In this day and age of swiping left or right, likes and messages, your spirit man needs to be in operation to seek the motives of what the individual or individuals you are communicating with really is being said. Remember, dating is the process of collecting data on that person.

I met someone over the phone and talked with him for seven months, which was seven months of unfulfilled promises and always wanting me to come to his place to hang out.

He never made any plans for us to go out, just for me to come to him. I made it clear he wasn't coming to my place, but I desired to be treated like a lady and go out to dinner, the movies, and other events; but it seemed that he just wanted to keep me his best-kept secret. I felt as though he wanted to keep me in the dark, meaning within the four walls or in the bedroom.

This man always made promises of what he was going to do as far as taking me out on a date, but it was always when he could get a day off work. People tend to make time for what's important in their lives. I realized I wasn't that important to him since he was full of unfulfilled promises that just became outright lies. He always told me what I wanted to hear. He never showed me anything but his character.

As I continued to communicate with this man, all that happened was me collecting data of what he wanted me to hear.

For his birthday, I cooked a meal and took it to him. It was nothing elaborate; it was just a brief drop off at his apartment. He tried to pressure me to stay the night with him, but that was not my desire, so I left, and right after this he became very distant.

In my wait, I need to maintain my commitment to God and the standards He has established in His word, so I could not fall for that temptation. I needed to protect my temple and my heart. Deep inside I knew this man was not the one God sent me, so I already felt that carrying on with the conversation was somewhat of a taboo, but I enjoyed the companionship, even if there was some contention in it.

Ladies, I had to be transparent in sharing this story because we are all tempted. This is why it's important to have your relationship with the Lord and to have His Holy Spirit because they will keep you grounded and bring back to your remembrance the promises, He has shared with you. Not only in His word, but the ones He has spoken to you personally. If He said it, it will happen, but in His timing and His timing only. Don't try to intervene and do God's job—He knows how to do it much better than you.

Holy matrimony is divinely blessed by God; God does not bless hook ups or one-night stands. One night of pleasure, and not even a full night (more like 20 minutes), has posed an open door for pain.

Remember what we mentioned earlier: the devil will speak your love language. He told me he was working overtime often so he could make enough money to move me into the dream home of my desire. I heard what he was saying, but as I listened, I just saw his character for what it truly was. I finally had to put a stop to all of it because I decided I was not going to play anymore games with men. And I realized he was just playing games.

God and I have been through so much, but in my trials and tribulations, I have gained God's wisdom. It is through His wisdom that I know the difference from God ordaining and the devil fabricating a situation. The temptations were so tempting, but I knew that I had to maintain self-control. The temperature of my heart had to be cooled, and to do that, I put a limit on our phone conversations and then finally just ended them. I knew that the best way to gauge the situation was to get closer to God and listen to the voice of the Holy Spirit. I realized that for seven months, I allowed the enemy to whisper in my ear.

Just know, ladies, when we stand firm in our "No" and make someone respect our "No," the ones who aren't for us will fall away without us having to do it on our own. We really can't do it on our own; remember Ishmael? He was a result of doing it in our timing while Isaac was in God's timing. God will close the door no man can open and open a new door no man can close (Revelation 3:7).

LOVE YOURSELF

After this situation, I went through a process of learning where I came to know what it is to love myself.

As I grew in love with my First Love (Jesus), God allowed a distraction to come to get my focus and my heart. I now see it was a test to see if my heart aligned to the heart of God. He was testing me because it's all about divine order, balance, and timing. This man is one who would have caused me to be unequally yoked, but God allowed me to talk with him for me to find it out myself. He was showing me what it looks like to be unequally yoked so I will know when the sent one comes.

The right now man, maybe just a distraction, an Ismael and not your Isaac. Sometimes God will allow your heart to be broken to save your soul. Ladies, we can't stay with "Mr. Wrong" while waiting on "Mr. Right". If you want what you deserve, you must keep your standards and remain an uncompromising woman of God.

IT'S OKAY TO LET GO

Doing the right thing is not always easy. I knew I had to let go, but in my heart, I truly liked the attention I was receiving even though I knew it wasn't from the one God has for me. My heart was tangled with certain feelings, but I also felt the Holy Spirit almost screaming to me, "HE'S NOT THE ONE!!!" The euphoria of the thought of having someone who was thinking of me captured my heart, and for a temporary time, it allowed me to tune out the voice of the Holy Spirit.

Thankfully, I came to my senses and tuned into the voice of the Holy Spirit and decided to heed the spirit's warning. Praise God for giving me the spirit of righteousness.

Ladies don't hold on to someone who doesn't align with God, someone who wants to keep you in the dark, because God has shined His light on your worth. Light can't be hidden by darkness; light illuminates the dark. Don't allow these men to have a hold on you, and don't allow any man to keep you waiting when he has made it clear you are his option, not making you, his priority. We deserve true love, and God says He will give us our heart's desires as we continue to delight ourselves in Him.

I saw the big red flags, but I ignored them because I was so focused on my desires to have someone in my life giving me attention. God even showed me in a dream that this man was not for me, and this is when I finally started to see it for myself and pull away even more. If he wasn't for me, why was I wasting my time? Time is one thing in life you will never get back, so we need to use our time wisely.

The men God has created for His daughters are from the king's lineage. Something must be going on inside of them that identifies with Christ. God is not only leading and guiding His daughters, but He too is leading and guiding His sons, so the man God has for you will be looking for the fruits being displayed inside your life and character.

TRUE LOVE WAITS

I want to share yet another transparent moment from my past of true love. I am sharing to encourage you that we can worship while we wait in God and on God with great expectations. He is a God who keeps His promises. His word will not return to Him void (Proverbs 37:4). Delight yourself in the Lord and He will give you the desires of your heart. I want to share with you all the benefits and blessings of waiting. God's love is truly an unconditional love that He gives to us all.

Before I was truly delivered from the spirit of lust, I had a weak moment. I cheated on my First Love (Jesus) with a man who was not God's chosen one to be my husband. I always wanted to please God in all my ways, and I did not want to play in the devil's den.

This affair was very short-lived, but it taught me to know my value and my worth. When God replenished me after falling into that sinful way, He cleansed me from that fall. He even took the desire away from me because I knew He was my source for all things. Praise the Lord! God is a deliverer!

I have been blessed by the Holy Spirit's help to present my body a living sacrifice holy and acceptable unto God which is (my) reasonable service (Romans 12:1). With the help of prayer, praise, and worship coupled with reading God's word daily, I've been blessed to stay clean now for over nine years. With the help of the Holy Spirit, my angels, my open and willing vessel surrendering to the spirit and an open heart to God, I have found it to be better for me to want what God wants for me. He's a keeping God if you want to be kept!

No Vain Waiting on God

I truly believe that our wait will not be in vain. But it is in God's perfect timing, and we must continue waiting in God and on God, and I know that everything will work for our good! Amen!

There is a difference between God's outlook on time and our own. Without beginning or end, time does not affect Him.

Writing the vision is very important. For the vision is yet for an appointed time, but at the end, it shall speak and not lie; though it tarries, wait for it, because it will surely come. Write the vision for your life and make it plan (Habakkuk 2:3); God will honor your desires as long as they align with His for your life.

Tarring is a Hebrew word that means "delay." It's used in reference to the Israelites as they were preparing to enter the land of Canaan. The Lord told them if they entered into His rest then they would keep His statutes (Hebrews 4:9). Tarry can also mean to delay or postpone something.

Did you know the reference to waiting is found in 116 instances within the Bible? Psalm 27:14, Micah 7:7, and Acts 1:3-4, just to name a few. In these examples, waiting was for the benefit of whom He was writing to. When God tells us to wait, He is doing it for our own good.

Merriam-Webster's Dictionary defines wait as "to stay in place until an expected event happens or until someone arrives or until it is your turn." To do something… or not to do something? Too often we understand waiting to mean we are wasting time or not taking charge of a situation. Biblically, waiting is an active verb indicating that to wait is to be aware through all the senses of what is occurring around you and discerning the right time to do or move to the next step. To wait is to be open to experiencing the holy moments around you to experience feelings emanating from another person; to hear words in a broader context; or to experience God's presence through others. By being in a hurry or just too busy with the wrong things, it is easy to miss these opportunities. Praise the Lord for wisdom to wait.

Ladies, if you don't have that wisdom, ask God to give it to you and then do the steps He tells you to take to obtain it.

GOD IS WORKING THROUGH YOUR WAITING

The virtue of waiting reminds me of when the baby is due, we know it's coming; however, we don't know the time or the hour of its arrival. Doesn't that sound familiar? We all know Jesus is returning, but we do not know the time or the hour; only God does. Waiting is a spiritual discipline because it allows us to experience more fully who we are, the world around us, and the presence of God.

Remember the dreams God gives you; He always speaks to us in ways we can understand. Decisions are thrust upon us, and the decisions that we choose to make are not always easy. The good thing is they can be changed.

I desire to remain faithful to my First Love (Jesus), ladies. We can hold on to God's unchanging hand to walk us to the altar when it's time. "*That good thing which was committed unto thee keep by the Holy Ghost which dwelleth in us.*" (2 Timothy 1:14 KJV) Cling to Jesus as a branch to a vine engraving God's word on the tablet of your heart. We've been given a great treasure—the knowledge of God and His Saving Grace—and it is worth holding on to and protecting.

And God gives us His Spirit to guard our knowledge with His Wisdom so that we do not lose hold of what we've been given. I found out that what I needed was right inside of me, and what I want is what God wants for me.

Make sure you have an accountability sister. Let others know that you have a date and who this person is because in this day and time dating can potentially be dangerous with so much human trafficking. Sis, never date in your home or his until God says it's time.

Be open with your communication regarding this topic because it's critical for your own well-being. Oftentimes, you may communicate your feelings regarding having someone in your home or going to theirs and their response would be, "I'm not going to do anything." What they need to know is even if they don't have intentions, I may have battles within, and by me saying this to them, it's protecting myself from me. Temptation is a battle that is sometimes difficult to overcome and if you place yourself in those situations you may succumb to the temptations; but if you are in a public setting it will be easier to overcome any temptations that come your way.

If you're doing things in order, everything will work out for your good. Remember, your waiting is not in vain; work while you wait in God and on God and ask God to show you your assignment. He has gifted you so use your gifts to help build the Kingdom!

IN CLOSING

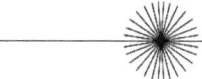

Prayer

Heavenly Father,

Help my sisters and give them strength and endurance to continue in the faith you called them to. I ask that you place people in their lives to encourage them. Give them a deeper love for you. Make them feel your presence and let them remember why they first loved you. You are our great Love, and you are worthy of more than we can give. Help us, God, to stay focused, and we ask these things in the name of Jesus! Amen!

One of the most priceless gems we will find in God's word is His voice. That's because He speaks to us through His word as we read it or hear it. We can't learn to recognize God's voice whispering to our soul if we are not first hearing Him speak to us in His word.

Let's practice waiting together, and may we be filled with God's Spirit as we are waiting.

It is my prayer that this book was a blessing to you. As I reflected, there were nine main points I wanted to make in this book for the single ladies. I understand dating can be difficult, but I also know it can be rewarding once the one God created for you has arrived. So, ladies, remember:

- Dating means collecting data.
- Only best friends can keep vows.
- Your standards should not be compromised.
- He should be responsible, empathetic, and intentional.
- Know what you need emotionally.
- Be super clear of your needs in a relationship.
- Don't fall in love with potential.
- Your needs should be his value.
- Ask him what he needs in his cup.

Remember, ladies, our emotional needs do not stay the same; they change, and so does his. Be supportive and do regular check-ins with your mate and ask if there is anything they need from you and let them know what your needs are as well. Communication is key; make sure you know your mate well enough so you can give him the love language that will satisfy his needs. Example, if you need more compassion, you should be compassionate towards him. One-sided relationships don't work, so be willing to give as well.

INSPIRATION

Sometimes we grow weary as believers walking the road of faith. From time to time, things do get a little difficult and hard, while other times it can get mundane. Sometimes doubt creeps in and we become weak when temptation arrives. We may even allow sin to fester in our lives and lead us to a place of complacency, ceasing us to listen to the Holy Spirit. As believers, we can encourage each other to continue in the faith; sometimes all someone needs is a reminder, encouragement, and support. Pray and ask God to connect you with a Holy Spirit-filled accountability sister.

ABOUT THE AUTHOR

Ms. Brenda Hunter Amponsah resides in Plymouth, Minnesota. She loves traveling, reading, walking, and enjoying outdoor events with her family. She has four adult children: one son, Terrell; and three daughters; Talisa, Jackie, and Sophia. She also has 14 grandchildren whom she loves so much. She enjoys going to family dinners and fun outings with her family. She loves attending Sunday School and Sunday Church Services as well as attending her quilting and sewing classes once a week.

Ms. Hunter is an ordained minister and loves the work she does with Women of Greater Hope and Vision Ministries, as well as being very involved in her local church, Spirit and Truth Worship Center, located in North Minneapolis, Minnesota under the leadership of Apostle Stephanie and Pastor Willie Bond. She cherishes her sisters in Christ who pray for her, support her, and uplift her as she is used by God to continue her journey.

MESSAGE FROM THE AUTHOR

As I began to build and work in God's kingdom for the last seven years, He has been using me as an outreach Minister operating in my own company (Women of Greater Hope and Vision) as the Executive Director of a nonprofit organization for domestic violence and abused women and those transitioning from Prison. It is a blessing to be able to do the work I enjoy as well as being available to those in need. I am blessed to be a blessing to many, and it's only because of the grace of God upon my life.

Thank you all for your time and for purchasing this book.

Sincerely,

Minister Brenda Hunter
God loves you and so do I!